CCMP™ Exam Prep
By Beth Kilgore

This exam guide is designed to assist in the studying efforts toward the Certified Change Management Practitioner certification (CCMP™). The guide includes robust effort towards different learning approaches, including 125 practice exam questions. This guide derives its information from the ACMP® Standard for Change Management© and ACMP Change Management Code of Ethics.

Table of Contents

Change Management - Process Group Order

Evaluate Change Impact and Organizational Readiness
Number 1-15 the order in which the processes occur

_____ Assess external factors that may affect organizational change

_____ Identify stakeholders affected by the change

_____ Assess the change impact

_____ Assess communication needs, communication channels, and ability to deliver key messages

_____ Define the change

_____ Conduct change risk assessments

_____ Assess organizational readiness for change

_____ Identify goals, objectives, and success criteria

_____ Determine why the change is required

_____ Assess alignment of the change with organizational strategic objectives and performance measurement

_____ Assess organization culture(s) related to the change

_____ Identify sponsors accountable for the change

_____ Assess learning capabilities

_____ Develop a clear vision for the future state

_____ Assess organizational capacity for change

Formulate the Change Management Strategy
Number 1-7 the order in which the processes occur

_____ Develop the measurement and benefit realization strategy

_____ Develop the stakeholder engagement strategy

_____ Develop the sponsorship strategy

_____ Develop the learning and development strategy

_____ Develop the change impact and readiness strategy

_____ Develop the communication strategy

_____ Develop the sustainability strategy

Develop the Change Management Plan
Number 1-4 the order in which the processes occur

_____ Review and approve the change management plan in collaboration with project leadership

_____ Integrate change management and project management plans

_____ Develop feedback mechanisms to monitor performance to plan

_____ Develop a comprehensive change management plan

Develop a comprehensive change management plan
Number 1-8 the order in which the processes occur

_____ Resource Plan

_____ Communication plan

_____ Sponsorship plan

_____ Stakeholder engagement plan

_____ Measurement and benefit realization plan

_____ Learning & development plan

_____ Sustainability plan

_____ Impact assessment and readiness plan

Execute the Change Management Plan
Number 1-2 the order in which the processes occur

____ Execute, manage, and monitor implementation of the change management plan

____ Modify the change management plan as required

Execute, manage, and monitor implementation of the change management plan
Number 1-7 the order in which the processes occur

____ Execute learning and development plan

____ Execute measurement and benefit realization plan

____ Execute communication plan

____ Execute sponsorship plan

____ Execute resource plan

____ Execute sustainability plan

____ Execute stakeholder engagement plan

Complete the Change Management Effort
Number 1-3 the order in which the processes occur

____ Design and conduct lessons learned evaluation and provide results to establish internal best practices

____ Evaluate the outcome against the objectives

____ Gain approval for completion, transfer of ownership, and release of resources

Change Management - Identifying Process Group Components

Match the sub process group to each process A-E

1. Develop feedback mechanisms to monitor performance to plan
2. Assess organizational readiness for change
3. Assess communication needs, communication channels and ability to deliver key messages
4. Develop a clear vision of the future state
5. Develop the sustainability strategy
6. Assess learning capabilities
7. Conduct change risks assessment
8. Develop the stakeholder engagement strategy
9. Develop the change impact and readiness strategy
10. Define the change
11. Identify sponsors accountable for the change
12. Assess the change impact
13. Gain approval for completion transfer of ownership and release of resources
14. Identify stakeholders affected by the change
15. Assess alignment of the change with organizational change with organizational strategic objectives and performance measurement
16. Develop the measurement and benefit realization strategy
17. Identify goals, objectives and success criteria
18. Assess external factors that may affect organizational Change
19. Assess organization culture(s) related to the change
20. Assess organizational capacity for change
21. Develop the learning and development strategy
22. Review and approve the change management plan in collaboration with project leadership
23. Develop the sponsorship strategy
24. Develop a comprehensive change management plan
25. Integrate change management and project management plans
26. Execute, manage, and monitor implementation of the change management plan
27. Modify the change management plan as required
28. Determine why the change is required
29. Evaluate the outcome against the objectives
30. Design and conduct lessons learned evaluation and provide results to establish internal best practices
31. Develop the communication strategy

A

Evaluate Change Impact and Organizational Readiness

B

Formulate the Change Management Strategy

C

Develop the Change Management Plan

D

Execute the Change Management Plan

E

Complete the Change Management Effort

Know your Definitions

Word Bank

Adoption
Benefit
Benefit Realization
Change
Change Impact
Change Management
Change Risk

Change Saturation
Competency
Current State
Engagement
Future State
Governance
Outcome

Readiness
Resistance
Resistance Management
Sponsor
Sponsorship
Stakeholder
Sustainability
Vision

1. An individual affected by a change. _____

2. The practice of applying a structured approach to the transition of an organization from a current state to a future state to achieve expected benefits. _____

3. A stakeholder's opposition to a change. _____

4. The ability to maintain the future state. _____

5. An event or condition that, if it occurs, may have an effect on the change benefits. _____

6. The quantitative and qualitative, measurable and non-measurable outcomes resulting from a change. _____

7. The individual or group in the organization accountable for the realization of the benefits of a change. _____

8. When the amount of change occurring in an organization is more than can be effectively handled by those affected by the change. _____

9. The decision-making processes, applied by authorized individuals or teams, for approving/rejecting, monitoring, and adjusting activities of a change management plan. _____

10. A specific, measurable result or effect of an action or situation. _____

11. Choosing to accept and demonstrate a new way of thinking or behaving. Adoption occurs when stakeholder behavior is consistent with the future state behavior. _____

12. How people, process, technology, and the workplace are affected during the transition from the current state to the future state. _____

13. The preparedness of an organization or its parts to accept, effectively handle, and integrate impending change. _____

14. The transition from a current state to a future state. _____

15. The organizational or individual collection of knowledge, skills, and abilities. _____

16. The description of the future state. _____

17. Stakeholder involvement and influence in the change process. _____

18. The condition at the time the change is initiated. _____

19. The process of addressing a stakeholders' opposition to a change. _____

20. The achievement of the expected outcomes of a change. _____

21. The condition at the time when the benefits have been realized. _____

22. The process of aligning stakeholders to support and own a change. _____

Know your Ethics

ACROSS

2. Duty of _____: Conduct yourself that consistently demonstrates your integrity
8. Duty of _____: Making decisions based on best interests of society.
10. Dimension advising to conduct all exchanges respectfully
13. Duty of …Supporting _____: Engaging in activities That enhance profession credibility
14. Duty of _____: Refusing to act in an abusive manner toward others
15. Dimension advising providing accurate information in a timely manner
17. Dimension advising earnestly seek to understand truth
18. Duty of _____: We do what we say we'll do.
19. Duty of _____: Acting with compassion and sensitivity

DOWN

1. Duty of Advancing the _____: Committing to share your knowledge to build consistency in value
3. Duty of ….Supporting _____: Enabling ongoing Education within the framework of the Standards of the ACMP for the profession
4. Duty of Advancing the _____: Supporting others through undertaking cutting edge research
5. Duty of _____: Constantly reexamining our objectivities and impartialities
6. Dimension advising to communicate genuinely
7. Duty of _____: Demonstrate consistent trustworthiness
9. Duty of _____: Providing equal access to info to those who are authorized to have the information
11. Dimension advising establishing relationships with frank exchanges based on trust
12. Dimension advising striving to create an environment where others feel safe to tell the truth.
16. Dimension advising to knowingly communicate with the intent to express truth

Practice Exam Questions

1. The individual accountable for the realization of the benefits of a change.
   a. Change Lead
   b. Project Manager
   c. Sponsor
   d. Stakeholder
2. This process focuses on development of high-level approach for change management with others on the project.
   a. Evaluate Change Impact and Organizational Readiness
   b. Formulate the Change Management Strategy
   c. Develop the Change Management Plan
   d. Complete the Change Management Effort
3. What should occur before formulating change management strategies and plans?
   a. Create the charter
   b. Obtain initial requirements
   c. Assess the risks
   d. Evaluate the effects and readiness for change
4. The resource plan includes
   a. Defining roles and responsibilities for the sponsor
   b. Creation of a staffing plan assigning individuals to specific tasks
   c. Which physical resources are needed for the change effort
   d. All of the above
5. Why is it important to manage individual and collective adoption?
   a. So stakeholders will be happy with the results
   b. To achieve expected benefits
   c. To ensure new ideas are innovative
   d. So stakeholders follow directions
6. Which have specific start and end dates?
   a. Project Management
   b. Change Management
   c. Both a and b
   d. Neither a or b
7. The _____ is responsible for coordinating, applying, and tracking change management tools or activities.
   a. Change Management Lead
   b. Data Analyst
   c. Project Coordinator
   d. Change Management Practitioner
8. What is the importance of alignment?
   a. Provides leaders clarity of purpose in times of change
   b. Increases likelihood of successful implementation
   c. Increases the likelihood of adoption of the change
   d. All of the above
9. What is a part of the first process for an upcoming change?
   a. Stating the case for change
   b. Detail the scope of the change
   c. Both a and b
   d. Neither a or b
10. Negotiating in good faith and treating others with dignity reflect which duty?

a. Duty of Respect
b. Duty of Fairness
c. Duty of Responsibility
d. Duty of Relationships

11. Elements of Change Management include:
a. Communication and Training
b. Stakeholder Engagement
c. Measuring Results
d. All of the above

12. Defining the change can include:
a. Whether the change is transformational or incremental
b. Identifying Goals
c. Identifying different levels of risk
d. Who needs to adopt the change

13. The case for change includes:
a. How many stakeholders will be needed for the change
b. The % of adoption needed for a successful implementation
c. Consequences of not changing
d. Which processes will be impacted by the change

14. Inputs used for defining the change include
a. Stakeholder analysis
b. Business case
c. External impact assessment
d. Risk assessment

15. Not understanding the reason for the change can lead to
a. Not meeting the budget
b. Additional objectives
c. Unsuccessful stakeholder adoption
d. Additional milestones added to the project schedule

16. Developing a clear vision for the future state takes into account
a. The strategic plan, business case, organizational chart, and research
b. The business case, organization mission, and strategic plan
c. Sponsor identification, research, and organization mission
d. The impact assessment, research, and business case

17. Manageable goals ultimately should represent progress towards the

_____.
a. Scope
b. Project Schedule
c. Risks identified in the charter
d. Adoption of the future state

18. Tracking change measures focuses on:
a. The change schedule
b. Change results and anticipated outcomes
c. Both of the above
d. Neither of the above

19. What is the difference between accountable or responsible stakeholders?
a. Those responsible bring the change to completion; Those accountable do the daily work of driving the change operationally to achieve its goals and objectives.

b. Those responsible do the daily work of driving the change operationally to achieve its goals and objectives; Those accountable bring the change to completion
c. Those responsible create the success criteria and work with the project team to adhere to the schedule; Those accountable oversee status reports and report to the sponsor.
d. Those accountable create the success criteria and work with the project team to adhere to the schedule; Those responsible oversee status reports and report to the sponsor.

20. What does the process *Identify Stakeholders Affected by the Change* entail?
    a. Determining the complexity of the change impact on key individuals
    b. Identify the level of influence and commitment for key individuals
    c. Identify those able to influence the outcome
    d. All of the above

21. What is the purpose of identifying stakeholder attributes?
    a. To determine which stakeholders don't have to adopt the change since they won't be open to it
    b. To update the charter with detailed stakeholder information
    c. To aide in preparing the change management strategy plan
    d. To ensure the organizational chart is correct

22. Which categories should the change impact assessment include?
    a. People, organizational structure, technology, change methodology
    b. People, processes, organizational structure, technology
    c. People, processes, technology, change methodology
    d. People, change methodology, processes

23. What are the 5 duties according to the ethical standards?
    a. Fairness, Responsibility, Respect, Honesty, Advancing the Discipline & Supporting Practitioners
    b. Advancing the Discipline & Supporting Practitioners, Honesty, Respect, Research, Responsibility
    c. Responsibility, Research, Respect, Retrospect, Reality
    d. Honesty, Respect, Responsibility, Advancing the Discipline & Supporting Practitioners, Reality

24. The impact of the expected benefits should be directly measured to _____.
    a. Vision statement
    b. Mission statement
    c. Organization's strategic goals and objectives
    d. Scope statement

25. Who should be included when conducting a review of strategy?
    a. End User
    b. IT team
    c. Program management office
    d. External resources

26. What are possible results of assessing alignment with strategic objectives for a specific change?
    a. Adapt a new strategy to coincide with the change
    b. Cancel the change if not aligned
    c. Postpone the change until it can be aligned
    d. All of the above

27. What are some external factors that need to be considered when assessing a change?
    a. Customer, political, social, human resource department
    b. Customer, market, social, legal

c. Economic, customer, human resource department, technology

d. Executive insight, market, social, political, legal

28. What is the definition of organizational culture?
    a. Shared values and behaviors unique to an organization
    b. Values adopted by the organization as a part of the vision statement
    c. Technical behaviors based on years of experience
    d. Thoughts and feelings of individuals of their current managers

29. Which assessment can be used to both anticipate and avoid possible roadblocks?
    a. Strategic assessment
    b. Impact assessment
    c. Culture assessment
    d. Predictive assessment

30. Why is assessing the capacity for change important?
    a. It identifies the current changes only, which helps to identify what can still be planned for the future
    b. It helps with deciding how much overtime to mandate for the change.
    c. It determines whether or not adoption is important for the change.
    d. It determines the ability of impacted stakeholders to adopt the change

31. An organizational readiness assessment will determine the organization's preparedness for:
    a. Change activities
    b. Mandatory adoption
    c. Renewing the vision statement
    d. Strategic alignment

32. What is an example of an input used for assessing the organizational readiness for change?
    a. Charter
    b. Vision statement
    c. Scope statement
    d. Status report

33. When assessing communication needs, the focus should be on:
    a. Communication needs of the majority of the stakeholders to build consensus
    b. Communication needs of all stakeholders, tailoring content to specific groups or individuals
    c. Communication needs of all stakeholders, with consistent communication to all groups or individuals
    d. Communication needs of the majority of the stakeholders, who should then pass the information to the rest according to their specific needs

34. Why is a risk assessment an input for assessing communication needs?
    a. It is used to determine risks that may affect communication effectiveness
    b. It is used to come up with one communication method that will work for all stakeholders
    c. It is used to determine risks that may affect the vision statement
    d. It is used to align all project team members to one goal

35. Which dimension of Duty of Honesty includes making commitments and promises, implied or explicit, in good faith?
    a. Candor
    b. Sincerity
    c. Truth
    d. Thoughtfulness

36. Which process focuses on which new competencies, capabilities, and knowledge needs to be obtained in order to achieve future state?

a. Conduct Change Risk Assessment
b. Conduct Readiness Assessment
c. Assess Learning Capabilities
d. Assess Culture Learning Capabilities

37. The change risk assessment should not only determine what risks are, but should also include:
a. Risk mitigation plan
b. Executive level agreement of risk mitigation strategies
c. Communication strategy associated with each risk
d. Measurement for each risk based on impact level

38. Which Duty is demonstrated by only accepting assignments that are consistent within your experience, background, skills, and qualifications?
a. Duty of Respect
b. Duty of Responsibility
c. Duty of Honor
d. Duty of Resilience

39. The change management strategy is typically tied to:
a. Organizational outcomes
b. Vision statement
c. Mission statement
d. Scope statement

40. Which process group documents feed the change management strategy?
a. Initiating
b. Determining the change impact
c. Evaluating the change impact and organizational readiness
d. Formulate the change assessment matrix

41. If the case for change is strong, why is the level of risk lower?
a. It indicates a technology improvement that will be easy to adopt
b. Those affected will understand the need and commit to the changes
c. A strong case for change requires a low budget, thus lowering the risk
d. The complexity is always low in a strong case for change which makes the change easier to adopt

42. What type of relationship exists between success of the change and clear and visible engagement from the sponsor?
a. Indirect
b. Relational
c. Direct
d. Obtuse

43. What is one way to advance the change management discipline?
a. Advising one another when approaching an assignment incorrectly
b. Creating templates for one another's assignments
c. Limiting the teaching of the discipline only to those who are qualified
d. Sharing findings of cutting edge research

44. What does a behavior change indicate?
a. An easier change since it requires managers to take control of their employees
b. An easier change since managing behavior is determined to be the easiest type of change
c. A complex change since employees do not typically listen to their managers regarding behavior changes

d. A complex change since behavior changes are harder to make compared to learning a new system or process.

45. Which of the following statements are correct?
    a. When customers or vendors are affected by the change, there is an increase in risk
    b. When customers or vendors are affected by the change, there is no change in the amount of risk
    c. When customers or vendors are affected by the change, there is a decrease in risk
    d. When customers or vendors are affected, it is impossible to determine the risk involved with them

46. Which area of misalignment in the change management strategy will negatively affect the change?
    a. Organizational structure
    b. Culture
    c. Performance management practices
    d. All of the above

47. What are elements of the communication strategy?
    a. General messaging, governance and review process, feedback channels
    b. Governance and review process, defined case for change, targeted messaging
    c. Identified channels for communication and feedback, stakeholders, risk assessment
    d. Targeted messaging, identified channels for communication, risk assessment

48. What does the duty of advancing the discipline & supporting practitioners entail?
    a. Refraining from using your expertise to influence the decisions of others
    b. Informing ourselves of the norms and customs of others
    c. Sharing knowledge to build consistency
    d. Disclosing potential conflicts of interest to appropriate stakeholders

49. When does successful communication of the case for change occur?
    a. Stakeholders can describe what is changing
    b. Stakeholders can describe how the change benefits the organization
    c. Stakeholders can describe how the change affects him or her
    d. All of the above

50. Inputs into the communication strategy include
    a. Change impact assessment, change definition, charter, stakeholder analysis
    b. Vision statement, change definition, stakeholder analysis, risk assessment
    c. Stakeholder analysis, vision statement, risk assessment, charter
    d. Change definition, change impact assessment, risk assessment, stakeholder analysis

51. What process does develop a clear vision for the future state fall?
    a. Formulate the change management strategy
    b. Evaluate change impact and organizational readiness
    c. Determine the clear path to success
    d. Understand the alignment objectives

52. Whom should be assigned the responsibility for developing the sponsorship strategy?
    a. Change management practitioner
    b. Change Agent
    c. Change project manager
    d. Change management lead

53. Sponsors provide resources and budget, set expectations and hold individuals _____ during the change.
    a. Responsible
    b. To a higher standard

    c. Accountable

    d. Hands

54. An organization has decided on a change, and has just finished conducting the risk assessment. What should occur next?

    a. Determine the learning capabilities

    b. Develop the communication strategy

    c. Integrate the project and change management plans

    d. Develop the resource plan

55. Creating a high-level approach for addressing sponsorship gaps should occur _____.

    a. During the implementation phase, since gaps won't be identified before then

    b. After implementation since adoption doesn't happen until the change initiative is complete

    c. As early as possible since sponsor engagement starts before implementation.

    d. Never, as gaps will not exist if the right sponsor is chosen.

56. The stakeholder engagement strategy should not only include the stakeholders whose jobs are impacted by the change, but should also include:

    a. Those who can influence the success of the change

    b. Family members of those who are impacted

    c. External vendors who lost the bid to participate

    d. The general public who are always curious about internal changes

57. What input(s) aide in creating the stakeholder engagement strategy?

    a. Change Impact Assessment

    b. Communication Strategy

    c. Stakeholder analysis

    d. All of the above

58. Establishing relationships with the expectation of forthright exchanges is called

    a. Respect

    b. Integrity

    c. Candor

    d. Sincerity

59. Once the stakeholder engagement strategy is complete, what strategy follows?

    a. Develop the benefit and measurement strategy

    b. Develop the change impact and readiness strategy

    c. Develop the learning and development strategy

    d. Develop the project management and change management cohesiveness strategy

60. What does the readiness strategy focus on?

    a. Actions and activities to be completed before, during, and after the change is implemented

    b. Actions and activities to be completed after the change is implemented

    c. Actions and activities to be completed during the change implementation phase

    d. Actions and activities to be completed before the change is implemented

61. What three learning requirements are needed for stakeholders to adopt the change?

    a. Knowledge, skills, and competencies

    b. The want to learn, know what the change is, know how their leaders are affected

    c. Skills, competencies, and relationships

    d. Knowledge, relationships, and skills

62. Which strategy includes the resourcing plan to conduct the learning and development activities?

    a. Communication Strategy

b. Learning & Development Strategy
c. Resource Strategy
d. Outsourcing Strategy

63. A two year long change implementation is in it's strategy forming process. When is the best time to deliver the learning and development of new skills?
    a. As soon as possible, as this will increase adoption.
    b. Before, but as close to the actual change as possible, so new skills can transfer to their jobs
    c. After the change is implemented, to make sure there are no surprise requirement changes that will impact the training
    d. Incrementally, with minor trainings occurring so as to build on each training prior.

64. What is the training content and measured adoption based on?
    a. Subject matter experts from each department, as well as from data and analytics
    b. Vision statement
    c. Learning objective (s)
    d. Mission statement

65. Measuring the change effort as early as possible provides the following benefits
    a. Allows for course correction, keeps the change implementation on track, ensures the organizational benefits in the project charter are realized
    b. Keeps the change implementation on track, ensures the outcomes listed in the change management charter are realized, allows the effectiveness of the change strategy to be gauged
    c. Gauges the effectiveness of the change strategy, keeps implementation on track, allows for slippage in adoption since adoption doesn't start until the end of the change effort
    d. Allows for course correction, gauges the effectiveness of the change strategy, ensures the outcomes from the change management charter are realized

66. Change objectives and goals are used to determine what is required to achieve future state. These measures should be:
    a. Qualitative and specific
    b. Qualitative and general
    c. Quantitative and general
    d. Quantitative and specific

67. Which duty is demonstrated through accountability while pursuing excellence and responding to expectations?
    a. Duty of Respect
    b. Duty of Responsibility
    c. Duty of Fairness
    d. Duty of Integrity

68. When creating a benefit realization strategy, components should include:
    a. Assigning owners for each measure
    b. Assigning owners for each target
    c. Establishing timelines for addressing issues related to achieving the targets
    d. All of the above

69. Once the change is implemented, it should become embedded in the organization. This is called:
    a. Change success
    b. Closing
    c. Sustainability
    d. Change strategic success

70. After the change has been implemented, the sustainability strategy activities are in place. These activities include:
    a. Monitoring the project scope for changes in objectives
    b. Knowledge transfer
    c. Updating the schedule to include activities that were missed
    d. Communication activities related to introducing the change to the organization
71. Once the strategies for the change effort are in place, the change management plan should be developed. This includes
    a. How to facilitate the change effort
    b. Creating guiding principles for communications
    c. Identifying sponsors accountable for the change
    d. Define the skills needed for stakeholders to adopt the change
72. In what plan does a gap analysis identify if the skills needed to adopt the change are missing?
    a. Communication plan
    b. Stakeholder engagement plan
    c. Learning and development plan
    d. Resource plan
73. What are the different types of resources to be considered in the resource plan?
    a. Staffing, budget, equipment, change management approach
    b. Human, physical, financial
    c. Human, equipment, budget
    d. Equipment, budget, change management approach
74. This plan identifies how to identify, develop, and strengthen the competencies required to lead or sponsor a change initiative.
    a. Learning and Development plan
    b. Sponsorship plan
    c. Stakeholder engagement plan
    d. Communication plan
75. The sponsorship plan includes
    a. Definition of specific responsibilities for sponsors
    b. Learning and development plan for the sponsors
    c. Consensus by the sponsors with how they will work with others engaged in the change activity
    d. All of the above
76. If a potential conflict of interest exists in managing or leading a change, the duty of fairness requires refraining from engaging in the decision-making process unless:
    a. You are sure your decision will not affect the project negatively
    b. Full disclosure has been made to the affected stakeholders including a mitigation plan and consent to proceed
    c. It is never ok to make decisions when a conflict of interest exists
    d. If the decision is not in favor of the conflict of interest
77. A stakeholder analysis identifies gaps from current state to future state in regards to stakeholders. The stakeholder engagement plan:
    a. Provides the activities to close the gaps
    b. Identifies the key components of those gaps
    c. Provides why the stakeholder will react to the future state
    d. All of the above
78. Which of the factors below should be considered in a stakeholder engagement plan?
    a. Activities that will keep a stakeholder attention

b. Organizational culture
c. Other change initiatives affecting the stakeholder
d. All of the above

79. Stakeholder engagement activities and sponsorship plan activities should be aligned because:
   a. When differing messages are received, it can be beneficial to see different view points from each level of communication
   b. Messages can be more clear and holistic if the messaging is consistent
   c. It will affect the change effort negatively if the sponsor sends out their communication before other influential stakeholders
   d. Influential stakeholders should always do what sponsors do

80. _____ communication activities include messaging around the case for change, why the change is occurring, and the risks of a failed change effort.
   a. Change
   b. Project
   c. Strategic
   d. Tactical

81. _____ communication activities include messaging around status reports and 'how to' guides for technology changes.
   a. Change
   b. Project
   c. Strategic
   d. Tactical

82. A key component of the communication plan includes defining what the audience should know, think and do because of the communication actions. This is called
   a. Key messages
   b. Timing
   c. Monitoring and Feedback
   d. Outcomes

83. Identifying audiences in order to group according to differing communication needs is a part of identifying the
   a. Key messages
   b. Reviewers and approvers
   c. Target audience
   d. Communication channels

84. Key messages in communication are identified as
   a. Words and visuals that will drive achievement of intended communication
   b. Important communications designed to drive the overall stakeholder adoption effort
   c. Messages from the change management practitioner about the status of the change management effort
   d. Communication from the sponsor on status of the change management effort

85. The role of the reviewer and approver in the communication plan is
   a. Review and approve the communication plan
   b. Review and approve the messages sent out to all of the stakeholders
   c. Review and approve the approach to the sponsorship strategy
   d. Review and approve the approach to activities that follow the feedback plan

86. How often should the learning and development plan be assessed?
   a. At the beginning and middle of the change effort (2 times)
   b. Continuously
   c. At the beginning since the training materials will not change

      d. At the beginning, middle, and right before the change implementation (3 times)

87. The measuring and benefit realization plan creates activities to provide valid and reliable data for tracking activity and effects on _____..
      a. Performance
      b. Knowledge
      c. Competencies
      d. Tactical skills

88. The sustainability plan includes the following components:
      a. Persuasive communication
      b. Incentives to reinforce desired behaviors and attitudes
      c. Implementing improvements based on feedback
      d. All of the above

89. Integrating the change management plan and project management plan
      a. Should look the same for every change effort to maintain consistency in the PMO
      b. Can be different dependent on the nature of the change program
      c. Should always be a different process since no change is the same
      d. Should occur after the governance structure is established

90. When it comes to sharing tools and resources between change management and project management plans
      a. It is best to use all of the same tools to maintain consistency
      b. It is best to use none of the same tools to avoid confusion
      c. It is best practice to look for opportunities of using the same tools for a holistic approach
      d. It is best practice to look for opportunities of using the same tools to save the company money

91. The responsibility of monitoring the change management plan belongs to
      a. Sponsor
      b. Project manager and change management practitioner
      c. Change management lead
      d. Change management practitioner

92. Respecting the property rights of others falls under the Duty of:
      a. Honesty
      b. Respect
      c. Responsibility
      d. Fairness

93. Benefits of reviewing and approving the change management plan in collaboration with project leadership includes the alignment of work plans, avoid duplication of efforts, and
      a. Increase stakeholder awareness
      b. Consistency in measuring the same success criteria
      c. Knowledge of approach methodology
      d. Increase modalities of feedback

94. Developing mechanisms for feedback and monitoring performance to plan may result in updated
      a. Communication plans
      b. Learning and development plans
      c. Measurement and benefit realization plans
      d. All of the above

95. Executing the change management plan includes
      a. Performing the change activities
      b. Monitoring and controlling the delivery against baseline plans

    c. Measuring against baseline plans

    d. All of the above

96. During execution, the budget

    a. Must remain consistent throughout the life of the project so as not to overspend

    b. May need to be evaluated for an increase, decrease or reallocation

    c. Is a guiding principle to follow if some activities need to be skipped to remain on budget

    d. Controlled by the executive sponsor

97. If a resource availability conflict occurs due to an unavoidable circumstance, the resource should

    a. Not be replaced. A lot of work goes into identify the resource capable of performing the work. The work can be completed once the resource is back

    b. Be replaced immediately due to lack of commitment

    c. Be reviewed for possible alternatives based on time availability

    d. Be reviewed for possible alternatives based on role identification, skill set, and engagement durations.

98. Which type of resources involve a process for creating, storing, and sharing records?

    a. Human

    b. Physical

    c. Financial

    d. Information

99. Acquiring physical resources such as buildings, rooms, and technology for a change relies on

    a. Execute facilities management plan

    b. Execute physical resource management plan

    c. Execute supplier management plan

    d. Execute monitoring management plan

100. The feedback channels and mechanisms identified in the communication strategy are executed

    a. In the execute communication process

    b. In the execute feedback process

    c. In the monitor communication plan process

    d. In the monitor feedback plan process

101. Who provides the coaching necessary for sponsors to understand their role, responsibilities, and expectations?

    a. Change management practitioner

    b. Change management lead

    c. Change management team

    d. Human resources

102. Who provides the sponsor with regular updates on the change effort status?

    a. Change management practitioner

    b. Change management lead

    c. Change management team

    d. Project manager

103. Which component of the change management plan includes activities that ensure all stakeholders understand and adopt the change?

    a. Stakeholder engagement plan

    b. Awareness plan

    c. Sponsorship plan

    d. Learning and development plan

104. Managing resistance to ensure a successful transition to future state should engage _____.
   a. CEO
   b. Each individual stakeholder
   c. A good number of leaders
   d. A small number of leaders

105. Learning objectives for stakeholders should be consistent with the _____
   a. Project scope
   b. Project charter
   c. Project management strategy
   d. Change management strategy

106. Assuming full responsibility for our own actions shows
   a. Responsibility
   b. Respect
   c. Honesty in conduct and behavior
   d. Fairness

107. What are the two steps in executing the learning and development plan?
   a. Develop the learning materials and complete the logistics of the learning activity for each group
   b. Develop the learning materials and archive for lessons learned
   c. Develop the learning materials and create measurement criteria
   d. Deliver the learnings and measure the criteria

108. What are the next steps if the learning does not produce the expected benefits?
   a. Re-evaluate and either modify or remove learnings
   b. This will not be the case as this should have been vetted in the strategy planning
   c. Deliver the materials again and ensure the audience is paying attention
   d. Contact the manager of those who did not achieve the benefits and come up with a performance improvement plan

109. If measurements indicate low stakeholder adoption, who should this be communicated to?
   a. Project manager so as to update the schedule
   b. Change manager so as to update the schedule
   c. Sponsors and project leads
   d. CEO

110. When tracking and measuring, what should the benefits be measured against?
   a. Industry benchmarks
   b. Identified targets
   c. Baseline data from the previous year
   d. Current state metrics

111. What information helps with the decision to adjust the course of execution?
   a. Vision statement
   b. Change log
   c. Risk assessment
   d. Progress monitoring

112. What should the change management lead include in the report on status of the change?
   a. Good outcomes, upcoming risks, progress from previous period
   b. Progress from previous period, any current obstructions, potential barriers to progress
   c. All overcome risks, upcoming risks, all outcomes

     d. All risks, changes to the project charter, dependencies

113. Participation from the impacted business unit in order to gain input and agreement on measurement and results is important because
     a. It's helpful in facilitating the potential transfer of accountability and measurement after the time of the change practitioner's involvement
     b. It's helpful to show the change practitioner is not accountable for the measurement, but the impacted business unit is
     c. It shows alignment between the project manager, change manager, and the impacted business unit in regards to measuring adoption
     d. It is needed for the impacted business unit to continue working with the project manager after the change manager is finished executing the plan

114. Executing the sustainability plan should include activities for the following component(s)
     a. Rewards and recognition
     b. Continuous improvement
     c. Sustaining ownership
     d. All of the above

115. At what point in the change effort may the change management plan be required?
     a. After implementation before measurements can be finalized
     b. After implementation and after measurements have finalized
     c. Throughout the life of the effort utilizing tracked measures according to targets
     d. Only after a change log records a scope change

116. What does complete the change management effort entail?
     a. Closing out the project and documenting lessons learned
     b. Transitioning to maintenance or sustaining activities
     c. Adoption is complete and there is no need to monitor for sustainment
     d. The project manager has signed off on the closing document

117. What actions are required to evaluate outcomes against the objectives?
     a. Compare outcomes of the change management effort against the change objectives
     b. Compare outcomes of the change management effort against project or program objectives
     c. Document the outcome comparisons with indicating whether objectives were not met, met, or exceeded.
     d. All of the above

118. How should one approach those persons with whom we have a conflict or disagreement?
     a. Through a mediator
     b. Through an arbitrator
     c. Directly
     d. Indirectly

119. What enables two-way feedback regarding how the change was embedded in the organization and regarding future improvements for change leads and the organization?
     a. Lessons learned
     b. Knowledge sharing sessions
     c. Closing document
     d. Sustainment document

120. Lessons learned evaluation activities include
     a. Identify and recognize positive outcomes
     b. Review change management activities and documents
     c. Verify and document actions for future projects

d. All of the above

121. The purpose of bringing people together for lessons learned evaluation is to:
   a. Review the change management objectives
   b. Review the effectiveness of the approach and ways of working
   c. Identify good outcomes and points for improvement
   d. All of the above

122. Where should approval be granted from for the completion?
   a. Stakeholder steering committee, senior sponsor, or client
   b. All stakeholders
   c. Project manager
   d. Change management lead

123. What are characteristics of strong change agents?
   a. Leadership, interpersonal, emotional intelligence, and communication skills
   b. Leadership, animated, communication, and project management skills
   c. Leadership, interpersonal, communication, and project management skills
   d. Leadership, interpersonal, emotional intelligence, extrovert, and communication skills

124. Doing what we say we will do is a component of the Duty of
   a. Fairness
   b. Respect
   c. Responsibility
   d. Integrity

125. The avoidance of engaging in behaviors that might be considered disrespectful is an ethic under the Duty of
   a. Fairness
   b. Respect
   c. Integrity
   d. Responsibility

Answer Key

Answers

Evaluate Change Impact and Organizational Readiness
Number 1-15 the order in which the processes occur

__9__ Assess external factors that may affect organizational change

__2_ Determine why the change is required

__6_ Identify stakeholders affected by the change

__8_ Assess alignment of the change with organizational strategic objectives and performance measurement

__7_Assess the change impact

_10_ Assess organization culture(s) related to the change

_13_ Assess communication needs, communication channels, and ability to deliver key messages

__5_ Identify sponsors accountable for the change

__1_ Define the change

_14_ Assess learning capabilities

_15_ Conduct change risk assessments

__3_ Develop a clear vision for the future state

_12_ Assess organizational readiness for change

_11_ Assess organizational capacity for change

__4_ Identify goals, objectives, and success criteria

Formulate the Change Management Strategy
Number 1-7 the order in which the processes occur

__6_ Develop the measurement and benefit realization strategy

__4_ Develop the change impact and readiness strategy

__3_ Develop the stakeholder engagement strategy

__1_ Develop the communication strategy

__2_ Develop the sponsorship strategy

___7_ Develop the sustainability strategy

__5_ Develop the learning and development strategy

Develop the Change Management Plan
Number 1-4 the order in which the processes occur

__3_ Review and approve the change management plan in collaboration with project leadership

__2_ Integrate change management and project management plans

__4_ Develop feedback mechanisms to monitor performance to plan

__1_ Develop a comprehensive change management plan

Develop a comprehensive change management plan
Number 1-8 the order in which the processes occur

__1_ Resource Plan

__4_ Communication plan

__2_ Sponsorship plan

__3_ Stakeholder engagement plan

__7_ Measurement and benefit realization plan

__6_ Learning & development plan

__8_ Sustainability plan

__5_ Impact assessment and readiness plan

Execute the Change Management Plan
Number 1-2 the order in which the processes occur

__1_ Execute, manage, and monitor implementation of the change management plan

__2_ Modify the change management plan as required

Execute, manage, and monitor implementation of the change management plan
Number 1-7 the order in which the processes occur

__5_ Execute learning and development plan

__6_ Execute measurement and benefit realization plan

__2_ Execute communication plan

__3_ Execute sponsorship plan

__1_ Execute resource plan

__7_ Execute sustainability plan

__4_ Execute stakeholder engagement plan

Complete the Change Management Effort
Number 1-3 the order in which the processes occur

__2_ Design and conduct lessons learned evaluation and provide results to establish internal best practices

__1_ Evaluate the outcome against the objectives

__3_ Gain approval for completion, transfer of ownership, and release of resources

Answers
Change Management - Identifying Process Group Components
Match the sub process group to each process A-E

1. Develop feedback mechanisms to monitor performance to plan **C**
2. Assess organizational readiness for change **A**
3. Assess communication needs, communication channels and ability to deliver key messages **A**
4. Develop a clear vision of the future state **A**
5. Develop the sustainability strategy **B**
6. Assess learning capabilities **A**
7. Conduct change risks assessment **A**
8. Develop the stakeholder engagement strategy **B**
9. Develop the change impact and readiness strategy **B**
10. Define the change **A**
11. Identify sponsors accountable for the change **A**
12. Assess the change impact **A**
13. Gain approval for completion transfer of ownership and release of resources **E**
14. Identify stakeholders affected by the change **A**
15. Assess alignment of the change with organizational change with organizational strategic objectives and performance measurement **A**
16. Develop the measurement and benefit realization strategy **B**
17. Identify goals, objectives and success criteria **A**
18. Assess external factors that may affect organizational Change **A**
19. Assess organization culture(s) related to the change **A**
20. Assess organizational capacity for change **A**
21. Develop the learning and development strategy **B**
22. Review and approve the change management plan in collaboration with project leadership **C**
23. Develop the sponsorship strategy **B**
24. Develop a comprehensive change management plan **C**
25. Integrate change management and project management Plans **C**
26. Execute, manage, and monitor implementation of the change management plan **D**
27. Modify the change management plan as required **D**
28. Determine why the change is required **A**
29. Evaluate the outcome against the objectives **E**
30. Design and conduct lessons learned evaluation and provide results to establish internal best practices **E**
31. Develop the communication strategy **B**

A

Evaluate Change Impact and Organizational Readiness

B

Formulate the Change Management Strategy

C

Develop the Change Management Plan

D

Execute the Change Management Plan

E

Complete the Change Management Effort

Know your Definitions Answers

1. Stakeholder
2. Change Management
3. Resistance
4. Sustainability
5. Change Risk
6. Benefit
7. Sponsor
8. Change Saturation
9. Governance
10. Outcome
11. Adoption
12. Change Impact
13. Readiness
14. Change
15. Competency
16. Vision
17. Engagement
18. Current State
19. Resistance Management
20. Benefit Realization
21. Future State
22. Sponsorship

Know Your Ethics Answers

Practice Exam Answers

1	c	31	a	61	a
2	b	32	b	62	b
3	d	33	b	63	b
4	d	34	a	64	c
5	b	35	b	65	a
6	a	36	c	66	d
7	d	37	d	67	b
8	d	38	b	68	d
9	d	39	a	69	c
10	a	40	c	70	b
11	d	41	b	71	a
12	a	42	c	72	d
13	c	43	d	73	b
14	b	44	d	74	b
15	c	45	a	75	d
16	b	46	d	76	b
17	d	47	b	77	a
18	b	48	c	78	d
19	b	49	d	79	b
20	d	50	a	80	c
21	c	51	b	81	d
22	b	52	d	82	d
23	a	53	c	83	c
24	c	54	b	84	a
25	c	55	c	85	a
26	d	56	a	86	b
27	b	57	d	87	a
28	a	58	c	88	d
29	c	59	b	89	b
30	d	60	d	90	c

<u>Practice Exam Answers continued</u>

91	c	**121**	d
92	b	**122**	a
93	a	**123**	a
94	d	**124**	c
95	d	**125**	b
96	b		
97	d		
98	d		
99	b		
100	a		
101	c		
102	b		
103	a		
104	c		
105	d		
106	c		
107	a		
108	a		
109	c		
110	b		
111	d		
112	b		
113	a		
114	d		
115	c		
116	b		
117	d		
118	c		
119	a		
120	d		

Made in United States
Troutdale, OR
10/12/2023